I Am a Good Friend

Sharon Coan, M.S.Ed.

These are my friends.

We like each other.

We help each other.

We **share**.

We talk and **listen**.

We play.

We care for each other.

We are good friends.

Make It!

1. Make a card for a friend.

2. Draw what you like to do together.

3. Write *You are a good friend.*

4. Sign your name.

Glossary

listen—to hear and pay attention

share—to use things with other people

Index

care, 14

help, 6

listen, 10

play, 12

share, 8

Your Turn!

Who is your friend?
Why are you friends?
Tell your friend.

Consultants

Shelley Scudder
Gifted Teacher
Broward County Schools

Caryn Williams, M.S.Ed.
Madison County Schools
Huntsville, AL

Publishing Credits

Conni Medina, M.A.Ed., *Managing Editor*
Lee Aucoin, *Creative Director*
Torrey Maloof, *Editor*
Lexa Hoang, *Designer*
Stephanie Reid, *Photo Editor*
Rachelle Cracchiolo, M.S.Ed., *Publisher*

Teacher Created Materials

5301 Oceanus Drive
Huntington Beach, CA 92649-1030
http://www.tcmpub.com

ISBN 978-1-4333-7345-9

© 2014 Teacher Created Materials, Inc.